IAN EDWARDS

Tales
from the Forest

Published in 2011 by

Royal
Botanic Garden
Edinburgh

20A Inverleith Row, Edinburgh EH3 5LR, UK

ISBN: 978-1-906129-76-7

The Royal Botanic Garden Edinburgh (RBGE) is a charity registered in Scotland (number SC007983) and is supported by the Scottish Government Rural and Environment Science and Analytical Services. RBGE is actively involved in projects relating to the research and conservation of the flora of forests across the world as part of its mission statement 'to explore and explain the world of plants for a better future.' To find out more about RBGE's work visit www.rbge.org.uk

The publisher acknowledges the support of the Forestry Commission Scotland towards the publication of this book.

Forestry Commission Scotland
Coimisean na Coilltearachd Alba

INTERNATIONAL YEAR
OF FORESTS · 2011

Designed by RBGE
Printed by Isafoldar, Iceland on FSC and PEFC certified paper
Text © Ian Edwards
Illustrations by Eri Griffin © RBGE

Contents

This book is dedicated to Stanley Robertson,
Scottish Storyteller (1940–2009)

Introduction

Why Tales from the Forest?

Stories form an important part of our lives and storytelling is what we do whenever we sit down to enjoy the company of others. Stories are used to sell everything from cars to chocolates; stories are used to educate, to influence and to entertain; and even in our digital age, stories remain firmly at the centre of our culture. You need only look at the Sunday colour supplements or advertising hoardings beside a busy road to see that trees and woodlands feature as prominently in the modern world of mass media as they did in the traditional tales told by the fireside in days gone by. There is no doubt that forest stories have always featured prominently in popular culture, but why do humans associate themselves so closely with trees and woods?

We could argue that our culture emerged from the woods. The first tribes who migrated northwards into the British Isles from mainland Europe discovered a forest that stretched from coast to coast and supplied them with all their needs – edible nuts, roots and fruits, as well as wild animals for meat and skins for clothing. These were available in sufficient quantities for people, at least in small numbers, to survive in the far north-west corner of the continent. I have lived with people who still live this close to nature in remote corners of the world and I have taken part in hunting trips with men armed only with bows and arrows.

As a lifestyle it is not particularly easy and requires much skill, ingenuity and courage, but it was learning to meet the challenges of a wooded environment that helped us develop into the highly versatile creatures we have become.

Within all societies certain plants and animals have a cultural significance which places them above the ordinary. In all continents it is possible to find trees, especially, that we have traditionally treated with tremendous respect. Generally this does not stop people using the same tree species for medicine, food, shelter or any other particular need but exploitation is usually controlled and the habitat managed in order to ensure the long-term conservation and sustainable use of the resource. It is only when respect for trees and woods declines, perhaps because an alternative material becomes available, that this relationship will break down and the woods themselves may diminish.

Our ancestors in northern Europe shared this respect for the trees and forests on which they depended. Forest animals such as the bear and the deer would have had their cults and particular trees, such as oak, ash and yew, were attributed with important, sometimes supernatural, powers. The ways of the ancient shamans or druids will probably always remain a mystery but the surviving tree lore, passed down to us by countless generations of rural inhabitants and travellers, must have been part of a forest-based culture that upheld the principles of conservation and the sanctity of life.

For a long time I have been fascinated by how the knowledge on which our relationship with trees and woods depends is transferred between generations, especially in parts of the world or in times long ago in which people could not rely on the written word. Imitation of parents or grandparents is clearly an important factor. I have watched small boys of only six or seven years old shoot little birds with toy bows that are perfect miniature versions of the ones used with such deadly efficiency by their fathers. I have also been taught to weave intricate baskets from palm leaves by young girls who have never been to school or had a formal lesson in their lives. They have learned mainly by watching and following the examples of their elders. Grandparents who may not take part in the hunt or foraging trips are often especially important in this respect.

Stories are also part of this teaching and learning process. Travel to any part of the world where television has not yet begun to penetrate people's homes and listen to the conversations that take place in the evening around the flickering flames of an open fire. Watch the animated faces of people as they recall the main events of the day, tell anecdotes and jokes, sing songs or tease each other. Traditional stories – tales that everyone has heard before, that have existed for generations and that are a mix of fact and fantasy – are often an important ingredient in this kind of gathering. The storyteller takes the listener into a world that may be familiar or, on occasion, to the very boundaries of belief.

I am in no doubt that stories help people make sense of and understand the world they inhabit. Often, however, what they are saying may be so subtle that the message is almost subliminal and, as in the cleverest advertisements, relies on repetition and familiarity to acquire mind space in the listener. The process can be very effective. It is not uncommon to find children in pre-literate societies who can name and explain the value of scores of species of plant or animal even though they cannot read or write.

Within our own British culture, however, stories making direct reference to trees or other woodland plants exist but they appear to be less common, at least in published collections, than in some other cultures, notably North America. Finding enough examples, even for this short collection, has not been easy and once or twice I have had to try to reconstruct a lost story from snippets of surviving folklore or parallels with similar stories from other places. I am uncertain whether this scarcity of stories is because our woods in Britain are diminished compared with those of mainland Europe or North America, or whether our northern neighbours have more woodland because of the survival of a forest culture.

When I first circulated this collection of tree tales among friends, colleagues and storytellers ten years ago I felt that I was throwing down a gauntlet and hoped I would receive letters and emails about important stories of native trees and forests that I had overlooked in my research. This hasn't happened but the challenge is still there. I hope by publishing and distributing this collection more widely it may encourage people to exchange stories with me and create a story bank that would be of great value to storytellers.

The nine stories I have included have all been written in a simple style that I hope will enable people to use them and adapt them for their own needs. I imagine them being told around a campfire, in classrooms or as part of a guided walk. They are offered with the proviso that they are told rather than read, thus returning them to the oral tradition from which they came. Confident storytellers will have no problem in making them their own. For novices there are techniques that can be employed to help learn a story and personalise it. The Scottish Storytelling Centre in Edinburgh runs a number of excellent courses for everyone from the total beginner to the experienced storyteller.

I have acknowledged my sources where possible and readers are encouraged to follow these up to get a different slant on the story. Enjoy telling these tales. They are not my stories, nor do they belong to those who created them back in the midsts of time: they are now your stories and by sharing them with your friends and others you are helping to keep a living tradition alive.

The Woman who Married a Bear

Years ago people, like the forest animals, depended
on wild foods such as blackberries, blaeberries,
sloes, wild cherries and hazelnuts for food.
Archaeology shows these were vital for the early
people in Scotland – collected in summer and
autumn and stored over the winter, they could save
a family from starvation. So when it was the season
for gathering a particular fruit, everybody, regardless
of their position in society, would join in the harvest.
But humans had to share the forest's bounty with

other woodland creatures, including the wild bears that lived alongside people in the Scottish forests until around a thousand years ago. By and large people and bears kept themselves to themselves but the following story, which starts with an unusual encounter between a bear and a human, is told in many different versions throughout the northern countries of the world.

One fine September day, the daughter of an important chieftain was out in the woods picking blackberries. As she worked among the prickly brambles she tried to take care not to tear or stain her clothes, but her mind was focused more on thoughts of her forthcoming marriage to a handsome young man from the neighbouring clan than on the task at hand. Suddenly, while leaning over to reach a particularly succulent bunch of ripe blackberries, she slipped and fell flat on her back. When she realised that it was a large pile of blackberry-stained bear droppings that had caused her downfall and, worse, that her fine dress was torn and covered in smelly purple bear dung, she let loose the most terrible oath. In the foulest of language she cursed not only the bear that had caused her misery, but the bear's entire clan – which had an ancestry as noble as her own.

Now, on the other side of the blackberry bush, unseen by the girl, two bears were peacefully gathering the same crop of ripe bramble fruits.

When they heard the young woman curse and
swear so coarsely and say such derogatory things
about their family they were very angry indeed.
They marched round to where she lay on the
ground, picked her up between them and carried
her back to their home where, kicking and
screaming, she was thrown into a dark cave,
and a big stone was rolled over the entrance.

She lay on the cold earth floor of the cave sobbing
for several hours. As the bears' captive she had no
idea how they would treat her and escape seemed
impossible. Then, amidst her despair, she heard a
high-pitched sound coming from a corner of the
cave. She stopped crying and realised that the
squeaky voice was talking to her.

"Well, this is a fine state of affairs," said the voice,
"a pretty pickle, to be sure."

"Who are you?" asked the girl.

"I am Mouse," said the voice, "and you must stop
blubbering for a minute so that we can think."

"Oh Mouse, it's hopeless," said the girl. "Surely I
can never escape from here, and who knows
what the bears plan to do with me?" For she
had only ever heard bad things about bears and,
dreadfully frightened, she started her pitiful
crying all over again.

"Do dry those tears," said Mouse. "I have a plan. First you must take your copper bracelet and break it into two."

"I can't possibly do that," said the girl, "for it is a symbol of my noble birth."

"Frankly, you don't have much choice, my girl. Now sooner or later they will remember you are imprisoned in here and when they open the cave to bring you food, this is what you must do. Ask to leave the cave so that you may relieve yourself in the woods. When you are done, cover it up with dirt and leave half of your copper bracelet on the ground where you have been squatting."

When the bear guards came they let her go into the woods to relieve herself and when she had finished she left half of the copper bracelet lying on the spot, just as the Mouse had told her to do. The guards returned the girl to the cave and the stone was rolled back into place, but not before they had discovered the copper bracelet on the ground where she had been. Now, in those times copper was a rare thing and fine pieces of jewellery were as admired by bears as they were by people, so the guards took the bracelet straight to the Bear Chief.

The next day the same thing happened. The girl was allowed to go into the woods to relieve herself and, following the mouse's instructions, she left the other half of the copper bracelet on the soil where she had been.

Although the girl was returned again to the cave there was a great deal of excitement among the bears. How could this girl turn prison food into precious copper? So she was brought before the Bear Chief for questioning.

"I feel I owe you an apology," said the Chief, "for I have heard of the miracles you have performed and I realise that you must indeed belong to a very noble family. I am deeply sorry I have treated you more like a slave."

The girl said nothing but raised her nose haughtily in the air.

"I mean to make amends," continued the Chief, "and anything I have within my power to give will be yours."

"The only thing I want is my freedom," said the girl.

"Of course," replied the Chief, "but first I want to offer you a gift as a token of my regret." As he spoke a servant came in carrying a beautiful soft pure-white bearskin rug and draped it around her shoulders.

Despite her anger the girl couldn't help but admire the quality and luxury of this beautiful rug and when she wrapped herself in its softness the world around her seemed to change. She felt quite differently about the bears that stood around her. Instead of seeing them all just as stupid bears she realised that each one was an individual. There were young bears and old, funny and serious, ugly and...

"Handsome!" she said to herself. "Yuck, how could I ever imagine a bear to be handsome?" And yet the tall young male bear who was seated beside the Chief did have a certain something which made him stand out from the rest...

As time wore on it became clear that although the bears treated the girl with much kindness and respect, the Chief had no intention of returning her to her family. Indeed, it became apparent that he had an entirely different plan for her, which was to be a wife to his nephew, the good-looking bear who sat at his right side.

Now, under normal circumstances it is unimaginable that a beautiful young woman of noble birth would ever agree to take a bear as a husband. But these were far from ordinary circumstances and it appears that the magnificent bearskin rug had magic powers, which meant the young woman saw the bears' world through very different eyes. The Chief continued to work on the girl, making all kinds of promises, until finally she could resist him no longer and agreed to a marriage with his nephew.

So the woman and the bear lived together, as husband and wife and part of the bear's extended family. They lived as bears do – on wild fruits and roots, with sweet honey and river salmon in season. Time passed and she came to accept, even to like, her new in-laws and to grow quite fond of her new husband, who was always good and kind to her. She missed her human family dearly, but whenever the aching sadness and longing became unbearable, she would wrap herself in the bearskin rug and the pain left her.

Then she discovered she was pregnant. The prospect terrified her and for the next months her mind dwelled on a single thought – what kind of offspring was she going to deliver? When the time came it was a great relief to her when she bore two perfectly normal and very beautiful twin boy bear cubs. And although sometimes she wished they would be a bit more gentle when feeding, she loved them dearly and devoted herself to bringing them up as useful members of the admiring bear family.

One day when the bear twins were two months old the bears heard a sound that sent a chill through the whole clan. In the distance they heard the baying of hounds, which the bear-wife recognised as the sound of her brothers' hunting dogs, and she knew that they had found her scent and were following her trail. Her husband consulted the Chief, who decided that to save the rest of the clan, his nephew and the

woman must flee with their cubs from their home
and fend for themselves as best they were able.

So the family left immediately but wherever they
ran, as night came and they made their camp, they
heard the barking of dogs – and each night the
pursuers sounded closer. Finally, when they were
so exhausted from the chase that they could run no
more, the bear-wife and her husband decided to hide
in a deep cave, hoping that her brothers would pass
them by. But when they awoke from a restless night
of sleep the dogs were right at the entrance of the
cave. At first light, she went out to negotiate with
her brothers. She knew they would never let her
husband live after he had abducted their only sister,
but they agreed not to smoke him out from the cave
but to allow him to die in ritual combat between man
and bear.

At the appointed hour the bear left the cave slowly,
singing a haunting lament, and as the brothers
circled around the bear, they were required to learn
his death song before casting the mortal blows that
brought him down.

The bear-wife returned to her human family and
married a man from the next village. In time the
couple had two, perfectly normal, human babies.
The bear cubs lived for a while in the village with
their mother but eventually decided to return to the
forest to be with their own kind.

Although this all happened a long time ago, this chapter in the history of bears and people was never quite forgotten. Sometimes, on winter nights around the fire, the old ones sing that tragic and mournful lament that was the final song of the bear who married a woman.

Notes

Stories of women taking bear-husbands are common and widespread among northern traditions. This version is based on the Haida (British Columbia) folk tale collected by Bill Reid and Robert Bringhurst and published in *The Raven Steals the Light*. Other stories on the same theme have been recorded in Finland, Sweden, Norway, Iceland and even Mexico! The best known Scandinavian story of a bear–human relationship is *East of the Sun, West of the Moon* which in turn is similar, and possibly derived from, the classical myth of Psyche and Cupid. According to Séamas Ó Catháin these stories are part of a circumpolar 'bear cult', which plays a fundamental role in the evolution of the Celtic ritual of Brigit, celebrated at the beginning of February. Even though the bear has been extinct in the British Isles for over a millennium the memory of this charismatic omnivore lingers within the folk tradition. In particular, the emergence of the bear following winter hibernation was regarded by the Ancients as highly symbolic of the rebirth and regeneration of the natural world. For a concise history of the bear in Scotland read *A Scottish Bestiary* by Francis Thompson.

Birch Maiden

A prince was out hunting in the woods with his hounds and men. The day was fair, their luck was good and they managed to bag a big, bristly boar. That night they camped by a babbling burn, under a graceful birch tree, with its sinuous, hanging branches reflected in the peaty-black water of a pool and shiny white bark that was broken by dark, diamond-shaped fissures. They feasted well on roast pork and oatmeal porridge and when they had eaten their fill they left the remains of their meal for breakfast.

Next morning the Prince was the first to awake and he had a terrible hunger. He went to help himself to some of the leftover food but to his irritation found somebody had beaten him to it.

"Who has dared eat before I have taken my breakfast?," roared the Prince, waking up all his men. They all denied having stolen the food and so it was a very grumpy and hungry party that set out for the hunt that morning.

Their luck remained good and on the second day they brought down a large stag. The evening was fine, with a bright full moon, so they agreed to a second night, roasting venison, drinking ale and telling stories, at the same lovely place on the river under the birch tree.

By midnight all the men were snoring apart from the Prince, who lay awake reliving all the highlights of the day's hunt. The fire had died down to embers but the moon was reflected brightly on the water and the silver bark of the birch tree. Through half-closed eyes the Prince saw the side of the tree open just wide enough for a slender figure to emerge. The Birch Maiden was dressed in a long white gown with a darker diamond pattern and in the moonlight the Prince thought she had the most beautiful face he had ever seen. Silently she crept to where the men were sleeping and then helped herself to the food that was left half eaten in their bowls.

The Prince rose quietly and took the Birch Maiden
by the shoulders, but when she turned to face him,
her deep brown eyes, which were fairer than the
moon itself, melted away any anger that was within
him. The Prince kissed the Maiden and held her in a
close embrace… and so they spent the night together
in each other's arms.

The next morning, despite having no breakfast
again, the Prince was feeling good. Of course he
promised to marry the Birch Maiden just as soon as
he had been home and sorted out his outstanding
affairs. He would return straight away to the castle
to tell his parents and begin preparations. She was to
expect him back before the next full moon and then
he would make her his bride.

How the Birch Maiden wept at the thought of her
lover leaving her so soon, and as he rode off with his
men and his hounds she cried through her tears.

"Remember to kiss no one until we meet again,
otherwise you will forget all about me."

The Prince knew that he never could but when he
arrived back at the castle he was very careful not
to let his parents or anyone else in the household
embrace him. He settled down by the fire to relate
his adventures to the rest of the family and his old
bitch, the mother or grandmother of all his hunting
hounds, came in. Seeing her master returned from

the hunt she went to him and gave him a big,
welcoming lick on his face, and from that moment
he forgot all about the Birch Maiden.

Although he knew not the cause, a great sadness came
over the Prince and he felt an empty longing which left
him feeling very ill. He took to his bed and the King
and Queen called the royal physicians to attend the
sick Prince, but none of their charms or potions were
able to heal him and he got steadily worse. The King
and Queen were distraught as they saw their only son
pine away. They put out a royal decree offering a rich
reward for any doctor in the land who could cure their
son. Many tried but to no avail. The Prince got worse
and worse until there was hardly any life within him.

Meanwhile, after her night of passion with the Prince,
the Birch Maiden tried to return to her tree but it would
not open to admit her. What had changed she could
not tell but it was clear that she was homeless and had
no choice but to seek her Prince. She arrived in due
course at the castle gates but she was told the Prince
was very ill and not fit to see visitors. So she cut her
hair short and bought a man's cloak, and so disguised
returned to the castle gates claiming to be a healer who
had come to cure the Prince. The guards were reluctant
to let her in, saying that the best physicians in the
land had already failed, so how could he, a young
man fresh out of college, hope to do any better?
The Queen overheard this conversation, however,
and bade the guards let the young doctor try his best.

When they were alone the Birch Maiden tried to remind her lover of the night they had spent together under the birch tree but it was clear that he was so weak he could hardly hear her speak let alone remember her face. She reached into her cloak and brought out a small green bottle containing a tonic made from the spring sap of the birch tree. Carefully she opened his lips, and when he tasted the liquid he opened his eyes and, seeing her deep brown eyes, he remembered at once the peaty brown pool, the twisted birch and the beautiful Birch Maiden who was now there at his bedside.

So it was that after this the Prince and the Birch Maiden were married and lived a long and happy life together.

Notes

European and Scandinavian folk literature is full of stories about birch trees but I was unable to find anything within the Celtic tradition. So I have adapted a story from the Mediterranean, in which I have substituted a silver birch for the bay tree of the original! Birch was always considered a feminine tree in Scottish folklore – the bonny birken tree was Queen of the Woods – so making the birch dryad into a beautiful princess seems entirely appropriate.

You will find the original Bay Tree Girl story in Michael Caduto's *Earth Tales*. I have also borrowed vignettes from the classic Scottish fairy tale The Green Man of Knowledge, which is found in Alan Bruford and Donald MacDonald's wonderful collection, *Scottish Traditional Tales*.

Old Croovie

Jack was a kind and honest lad but his master,
the Laird o' the Black Arts, was as cruel as he
was mean. Jack tended the Laird's sheep from
dawn to dusk, and all for two pennies a day. But
despite the poor pay, Jack worked willingly at his

job because as shepherd he could spend his days in the countryside among the woods, streams and green pastures, under wide open skies, enjoying the company of wild creatures. He lived with his mother in a tumbledown two-room stone cottage. Every day the old woman would bring Jack his lunch and if the weather was fair she would sit with him a while spinning chunks of wool that the sheep had left on bushes and fences.

One midsummer's eve, Jack was out on the hill tending his sheep in a field above a huge oak tree known as Old Croovie, when something very strange happened. All the birds that had gathered on the branches of the old oak suddenly took flight. Jack, who understood the language of birds, heard them screech and cry and twitter as they flew, "We're off, we're off, tonight's the night, we're off!"

Jack waited for his mother to arrive with his lunch and told her about the strange behaviour of the birds.

"Once in 100 years, or so folks say in these parts," said Jack's mother, "Old Croovie oak and his pals lift themselves out of the earth and perform a strange dance. Jack, I think the birds are telling you that the trees will be dancing tonight!"

"Well, that really would be a rare sight," said Jack. "I will stay and watch."

"Do be careful," said his mother. "I fear there is great danger around on nights like tonight" and she thrust the ball of wool she had been spinning into Jack's hands and said, "Take this, Jack, you might need it, and do remember: no good ever comes to the greedy!"

Jack was just wondering what possible use he might have for a ball of his mother's homespun wool when Jeannie, Jack's sweetheart who worked as a maid in the big house, came running up the hill out of breath.

"'Tis the Laird o' the Black Arts," she said. "He is in such a peculiar state. He has got some wild notion about Old Croovie and has forbidden any of the servants to leave the house after dusk." This made Jack even more determined to stay around and watch what was going to happen, even though Jeannie, like his mother, pleaded with him to take care.

In Aberdeenshire at midsummer it hardly gets dark at all, but in the twilight hours around midnight, soon after the moon appeared above the horizon, Jack was woken from his doze by soft music playing, a sweet harp-like tune all around him. As the music got louder the birch trees on the other side of the valley began to sway in time to the rhythm and then, to Jack's amazement, they lifted themselves right out of the ground and began to waltz together down the slope towards the stream. Meanwhile, Old Croovie and the other oaks were stretching and lifting their branches, until with a loud tearing sound they too heaved their massive bodies from the earth, leaving their root holes behind, to join the dance.

Jack watched entranced as birch clasped oak, and oak birled birch around in a dance, which became wilder and wilder as the music got faster and louder. Then he saw the Laird o' the Black Arts striding down from the big house and heading for the grove of dancing oak trees.

"Be gone with you lad," said the Laird. "You have no business here tonight. Go home before I have you arrested for poaching!"

Jack had no intention of leaving, however, and he watched as the Laird went down into the biggest hole, the one left by the roots of Old Croovie himself. Then Jack crept over to one of the smaller holes and peered inside. When his eyes adjusted to the darkness he was astounded to see gold goblets, silver rings, jewel-encrusted bracelets and all kinds of wonderful treasures. Jack climbed down into the hole and looked around him.

Remembering his mother's parting words, he didn't stuff his pockets full but he couldn't resist gathering up a pretty little silver cup for his mother and a beautiful gold ring for Jeannie. Taking a small handful of jewels for himself he then began to climb out of the hole but every time he tried to get a grip the sides crumbled away. To his horror he realised he was trapped in the root hole.

At that point, whose head should appear over the edge of the hole but Jeannie's. "Jack, Jack, you must hurry," she cried. "The music is slowing down and I think the dance will soon end."

Then Jack remembered the wool his mother had given him. He kept hold of one end and threw the rest of the ball up to Jeannie. She held on fast as he began to pull himself out of the hole. Fortunately Jack was light, while the wool was strong, and so was Jeannie. Once Jack was on level ground they ran as fast as they could to Old Croovie's root hole where the greedy Laird was still stuffing his huge sack full of gold and treasures.

"Come out quickly," said Jack to his master. "The dance is over and Old Croovie is coming back."

"Be off," said the Laird, without looking up. "You'll take a drop in wages for your disobe...!"

It was too late. Old Croovie was already standing over the spot and with a great sigh of exhaustion he settled back down into his root hole, burying both treasure and the Laird o' the Black Arts, who was never seen again.

Jack went back to his mother's house and gave
her the silver cup and Jeannie the gold ring.
By and by Jack and Jeannie were married and
with the handful of jewels he had saved they bought
a bigger and better cottage which they shared with
Jack's mother. It was the Laird's son who inherited
the farm and he was a kindly master, increasing
his faithful shepherd's wage – to two-and-a-half
pence a day.

Notes

This is a very popular 'Jack Tale' from the Scottish traveller's
tradition. It is always credited to master-storyteller
Stanley Robertson from Aberdeenshire who died in 2009,
although I'd heard it told three times by revivalist storytellers
Kate Ainsworth, Claire McNicol and John Hamilton before
I finally tracked it down in Stanley's wonderful book, *Exodus
to Alford*. Here it is written in the Doric-Scots dialect of the
north-east. Like many traveller tales it has a strong moral which
is as relevant to our current attitude to the Earth's precious
natural resources as it is to more prosaic treasures. I am told
that the ancient Croovie Oak can still be seen today along the
Old Lumphanan Road on Donside. The name Old Croovie is
presumably derived from the Gaelic a'chraobh – the tree.

The Blaeberry Girl and the Fairy

Once upon a time a little girl called Alice went out
to the woods to pick blaeberries for her crabbit
old grandmother who lived alone in a tumbledown
crofthouse on the edge of the moor. As she picked
the fresh, plump blaeberries, she said to herself,
"One for the basket, two for the basket, three for the
basket," and then, "one for me, two for me, three for
me" as she popped berries into her own mouth.

By noon her basket was full, but she had eaten
so many berries that her stomach was too!
And, as you will know if you have ever eaten a
lot of blaeberries yourself, the fruit makes your
throat and the back of your mouth really dry.
So she went down to the stream to get herself a
drink of water.

As she leaned over the little tumbling waterfall,
holding out her cupped hands to catch some
water, she heard a funny little piping tune coming
from behind her. But as soon as she looked at
the place where the sound had come from, the
music stopped.

So Alice leaned over the stream a second time and
just as she was going to fill her hands, there was
the sound of the pipe again. She spun round but it
stopped dead. The third time she only pretended to
reach for the water, all the time looking out of the
corner of her eye, and saw a tiny fairy man playing
on his penny whistle. So as quick as a flash she
reached out and grabbed the wee man, who was
no bigger than her thumb, by his middle.

(Now, I really should explain about this fairy: it was
not the delicate, gossamer-winged type of fairy girl
you see on top of a Christmas tree. This was a real
live fairy man, one of the tribe of 'Good People',
dressed in a green suit and red cap and with a long,
white, pointed beard.)

"Let me go, let me go, let me go!" cried the fairy, struggling in Alice's hand. But she held him so tight he couldn't wriggle free.

Now Alice knew a thing or two about fairies, including the fact that they always have a crock of gold hidden somewhere. She also knew that fairies never tell a lie – for if they do they die. So Alice said to the wee man, "I will not let you go unless you tell me where you have buried your gold."

"I will, I will," said the fairy. "Just let me go."

"First tell me where the gold is hidden," said Alice.

"It is just over there," said the fairy. "Underneath that blaeberry bush."

Of course Alice knew that he was telling the truth, for if a fairy tells a lie it will die, but she thought about it for a while and said, "I believe you, fairy man, but I don't trust you. If I go back to my grandmother's croft to get a spade, you will dig up the crock and hide the gold somewhere else."

"Just let me go," said the fairy, who was now very red in the face, "and I promise, fairies' honour, that I won't dig it up."

Now Alice knew that he was telling the truth, for if a fairy tells a lie it dies. But she still didn't trust him.

"I believe you," she said, "but all these blaeberry bushes look the same. If I go back to my grandmother's croft for a spade, when I get back how will I know under which bush to find the gold?"

So the fairy man leaned over and untied a ribbon from Alice's hair.

"I will tie this around the blaeberry bush," he said, "so that when you return with a spade you can find it again."

"I'm not as foolish as that," said Alice. "When I am away you'll untie the ribbon and run off with it."

"Let me go and I promise not to untie the ribbon," he said.

Alice, of course, had to believe him, because fairies always tell the truth – if they tell a lie they die. So she ran off to her grandmother's croft to get the spade.

She came back breathless and straight away began digging under the blaeberry bush with the ribbon tied to it. But there was no crock of gold. Then she noticed the next blaeberry bush also had a ribbon tied to it... so did the next one... and the next and all the rest! The crafty fairy had used his magic to make a whole lot of ribbons and tied one

around every single bush. Alice never did find
his hidden hoard and when she realised that she
had been tricked she sat down and wept.

So it really is true that a fairy can never tell a lie
but that still doesn't mean they can be trusted!

Notes

I have only heard this story once – told by Martin Watssman.
Although it has become almost mandatory to say that 'real'
fairies are not like the popular image of tiny feminine things
with wings, I like to believe there are some that are! If you
are serious about fairies then I recommend you read an
entertaining and scholarly book on the subject by Diane Purkiss
called *Troublesome Things* or the seventeenth century Scottish
clergyman, Rev Robert Kirk's unique exploration of fairyland
The Secret Commonwealth of Elves, Fauns and Fairies.

Secret of the Fern Roots

There was a time when the rivers of Scotland ran clean from the source to the sea and the forest stretched from the coast to the mountains. In those days two types of people lived in the countryside. There were the village folk, who lived in houses, and another race of small, elusive beings who lived in the woods. It was said that these woodland dwellers understood the secrets of the Earth – knowledge they had discovered by reading the roots of ferns. But whenever village people tried to pull up fern roots they would always break. They hadn't discovered how to uncover them gradually, layer by layer, which could take generations.

The people who lived in houses envied the secret knowledge of the forest people. The forest people didn't envy anything their neighbours had but they were curious about their ways. Sometimes at night the forest folk would approach houses in the village and peep through the shutters at the goings-on inside. They were very careful not to be seen, however, and would slip away into the dark shadows of the night if they thought they were in any danger.

Although they rarely caught more than a glimpse of their neighbours, the village people knew they were being watched and decided to play a trick on the forest people that they hoped would teach them a lesson. That evening the villagers held a party with dancing, feasting and merrymaking, knowing that it would attract the inquisitive forest people. They danced and danced until very late into the night and then retired to their beds, leaving a single pair of clogs, tied at the laces, in the middle of the dancing area between the houses.

At first the forest people stayed in the leafy shadows, too afraid to come out. Eventually one brave young man plucked up the courage to approach the clogs. As the forest people always went barefoot, when he saw the shoes he thought that one of the village people had left a pair of their big clumsy feet behind! He picked them up, looked at them, sniffed them and then, very carefully, slipped his two feet into the holes.

The instant his feet touched the inside of the clogs they began dancing of their own accord. As he struggled to pull them out again the dancing got faster and wilder and he found himself spinning round and round, kicking his feet out in every direction. Faster and faster, wilder and wilder – there was nothing he could do to control his own legs! Terrified, his friends disappeared among the trees, but the village people got out of their beds to watch and began to laugh and jeer at the ridiculous sight of the little man dancing madly in the far-too-big clogs.

Just at the point when he was about to drop dead from exhaustion one of the village people clapped his hands and said "Stop clogs!", and they were still. Before he had time to regain his senses and slip back into the forest the little man was marched off to a byre where he was locked up for the night.

The forest man stayed a prisoner of the village people. Every day they would try to persuade or force him to teach them the language of the fern roots but every day he refused, knowing that the special secrets of the Earth are not for those who fear and imprison anything that runs wild and free. And when he felt his courage failing him, his wife would come at night and through the thin wooden walls of the byre she would remind him that the knowledge he had inherited from his parents and grandparents must never be given to people who would abuse it.

I would like to be able to tell you that in the end the little man came up with a clever plan and managed to escape his captors. That didn't happen. He remained their prisoner for many weeks until the village people realised he was not going to tell them anything they wanted to know. To be honest they'd had their fun and were rather bored with him by this point – so they let him go.

After this happened the forest people were very careful not to be seen. Oh yes, it is true that every so often someone claims to have had a glimpse of them in some lonely forest ride or shady clearing but they never come near houses these days. And the lost language of the Earth still remains a mystery to most of us – a secret written in the fern roots.

Notes

This French tale, *Le Conte du Secret de la Fougère*, was first recorded by Henri Pourrat. This version is based on a translation and retelling by Michael Caduto from *Earth Tales*.

Fern roots, or rhizoids, are very fine and delicate. To extract them from soil would take a great deal of patience! In many species they are shiny black and are used in some cultures as a decoration in fine ornamental basketry.

Labra the Mariner

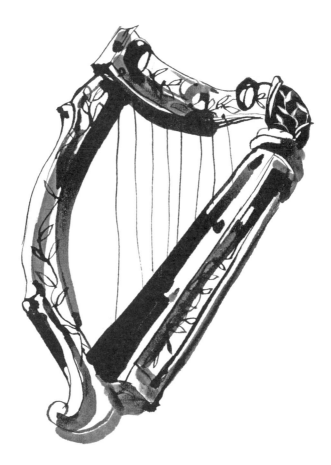

There was a time when kings who suffered any kind
of physical injury or deformity were not allowed
to rule. This is the reason that Labra the Mariner,
King of Ireland, went to such murderous lengths to
keep his secret to himself.

Labra was born with horse's ears, but these were kept carefully concealed beneath a large and elaborate crown. No one apart from his mother was ever allowed to know of the King's secret and anybody who found out – nursemaids, crown makers, barbers – was ruthlessly killed. As you can imagine, hairdressing ceased to be a very popular trade within Labra's kingdom, and when it was no longer possible to find a barber in the land, Labra ordered ordinary people from among the poor to perform his monthly trim.

The King was not entirely without a conscience, however, and when a poor widow pleaded for the life of her son who had been ordered to cut the royal hair, Labra relented on the understanding that the son be sworn to secrecy.

The boy was a good and honest lad but sometimes a big secret becomes just too great a burden to bear. When he could not stand it any more he went to a druid for advice and was told no harm would be done if he went to the woods and shared his secret with the trees.

He was very much relieved and when he left the druid's house he went straight down to the riverside where there was a grove of whispering willow trees, and he told them the secret of the King's ears. The willows seemed to respond with a faint sniggering and the boy left feeling much lighter for the weight having been lifted from his mind.

This is not the end of the story – for soon after,
a master harp maker went to the same grove of
willow trees, selected an especially fine specimen
and cut it down. The wood was sawn and seasoned
and eventually made into a very fine harp. It was
a magnificent instrument with a delightful tone to
match its exquisite beauty. A harp fit for a king!

So the willow harp was acquired by the Royal
Harper, Craftiny, who brought it to court for
the entertainment of King Labra. When all were
assembled Craftiny began to play but instead of
responding to the harper's fingers, the harp seemed
to have a mind of its own and began to sing in sharp,
clear tones:

> "The King has a secret, the Willows all share,
> The ear's of a horse poke out through his hair!"

The courtiers were astounded, but when they saw
the anger on the King's face, they knew the harp
was telling the truth and couldn't hold back their
laughter. But the harp continued:

> "Is this a time to shake with mirth?
> Remember those he put to death,"

and all fell silent, ashamed and angry with the King.

Now that Labra's secret was known to all, another
was chosen to rule the people. Craftiny continued to
play the willow harp, which proved to be the most

mellow of instruments, but it never spoke again of its own accord. And the widow's son grew to be a fine young man who was much respected within the royal court for his integrity and wisdom.

Notes

Poets, authors and storytellers have often alluded to the music that can be heard when the wind passes through the leaves of the willow tree. The acoustic properties of willow wood have also been appreciated by instrument makers and one of the oldest and finest of harps in Ireland has a soundbox of willow and a post of oak. No doubt the association of willow, representing femininity, with oak, dedicated to a male deity, was considered significant to the harp maker. There are many versions of this story; this is one from Alexander Porteous *The Lore of the Forest*. There are obvious parallels between Labra the Mariner, who is also known as Maon, and the Greek King Midas. The Cornish King Mark (see Tristan and Isolde) was also said to have horse's or donkey's ears.

Tristan and Isolde

Isolde, the fair daughter of the King of Dublin, was
not too happy about the prospect of marrying a man
she had never met, but her wedding to the Cornish
King Mark was seen by both families as an astute
political move, uniting two important Celtic kingdoms.
So it came about that Tristan, Mark's nephew, was
sent to Erin to escort the lovely Isolde to Cornwall.

Tristan was the natural choice for this task, which
was not without risk in those dangerous days of
pirates and bandits and even the occasional dragon.
Not only was he incredibly strong and brave, but he
also had a powerful charm which protected his life.

It could also be added that he was skilled at games,
a gifted musician and devastatingly handsome.

During their passage back across the Irish Sea,
the wind dropped and for days their boat drifted
aimlessly across calm waters. To pass the time
Tristan played Isolde soft airs on his harp and they
spent many hours over long games of chess. Days
went by slowly until one warm afternoon they sent
a page down below decks to fetch them each a glass
of wine. Instead of wine the page accidentally filled
their glasses with a powerful love draught, prepared
by the Irish King's herbalists and intended to be
drunk by Isolde and Mark on their wedding night.

Each took a sip from the charmed potion and,
instantly, they both fell hopelessly in love with the
other. How they spent the rest of the long sea voyage
we can only imagine but when they finally arrived
in the palace of the King of Cornwall the passion
between them had to be carefully concealed. The
arrangements for the wedding had already been made
and Tristan had to endure in silence while his true
love Princess Isolde married his kinsman King Mark.

This was not the end of the affair, however. Tristan
struggled with intense emotions: the conflict between
his loyalty and friendship for King Mark and his
deep longing for the lovely Isolde. The two lovers
met on secret assignations in discreet corners of the
castle and hidden from view in the wooded grounds,

but eventually they could stand the deception no longer. Tristan and Isolde eloped together, leaving Cornwall and fleeing to Scotland where they sought safety. In this far kingdom they lived in rustic bliss in a rough wooden hut deep within the heart of the Wood of Caledon.

It was none other than the great Celtic champion of the British, Arthur, who was charged with the task of tracking down the two lovers. When Arthur eventually found their leafy bower, he sent not men with swords and spears but bards with harps and songs to lure them out of hiding. This was a wise move, for if Tristan had encountered armed knights he would surely have slain them but when he heard the sweet music of the bards he was overcome with emotion. So the lovers willingly left their refuge to stand proudly before Arthur and his men.

Tristan and Isolde were taken to the court of the Cornish King to stand trial and Arthur, who was widely respected for his wisdom, was asked to be the judge. Witnessing the love between Tristan and Isolde, Arthur could not bear to part them, but at the same time he knew that Mark was the wronged party whose honour and pride had been deeply wounded. So Arthur cast the judgement that Isolde should be shared between Tristan and Mark, spending the months when the leaves were on the trees with one, and the months when the trees were leafless with the other. The King, as the rightful husband, was to choose first.

Mark thought of the long winter nights, when it was cold and grey and the castle seemed such a lonely place. Surely it would be best for Isolde to brighten his life when there were no leaves on the trees.

At which point Isolde let out a great whoop of joy. During her time with Tristan in the woods she had learned well the ways of the trees, and she cried out

> "Praise to the evergreens
> Holly, ivy and yew.
> To my loyal friends
> who stay green the whole year through."

So it was that because of this trio of evergreens (to which she might have added Scots pine if it had scanned properly) Isolde was allowed to wed Tristan and share his charmed life in some distant part of the kingdom, we know not where.

Notes

The botanist in me is intrigued to know what concoction of plants went into the love draught shared by Tristan and Isolde. I assume herbs were the main ingredients as they were in virtually all drugs until relatively modern times. Lime, with its signature of heart-shaped leaves, is the tree of love and produces flowers that make a delicious, honey-scented tea. Many other plants are reputed to have aphrodisiac properties but I like the notion of a lime flower cordial, made by Irish monks to sweeten the nuptial bed of the reluctant bride.

Merlin

Merlin is universally known as the wizard at the
court of King Arthur. However, historians may
dispute this and there is a notion that the real Merlin
(or Myrrddin) lived two generations after Arthur's
death and served another king, Gwenddoleu, one
of the last British kings to follow the old pagan
ways. In this version of events Merlin was a bard,
or possibly a druid. In 573AD, he followed his king
into battle at Arthuret, in north-west England,
against another minor British king, Gweddoleu's
distant cousin, Peredur of York. Peredur was a
Christian and the Battle of Arthuret saw a decisive

victory for the new religion over the old. By all accounts it was a bloody battle, with heavy losses on both sides. Traumatised by what he had witnessed on the battlefield, Merlin sought refuge in that part of the Great Forest of Caledon (Kelyddon) now known as Ettrick Forest, west of Selkirk.

It seems likely that all but the most remote Scottish forests had been cleared or damaged by Iron Age farmers long before the Romans reached the Border Country. The expanse of native woodland, however, fluctuated from century to century and forest clearance would not have occurred over the whole countryside. It is quite possible, therefore, that a substantial piece of wildwood survived in the southern part of Scotland until the 6th century. If this was the case then it would have been the perfect hiding place for a half-crazed druid because, from what little we know of the old pagan religion, it appears that woods and trees were as highly esteemed by our ancient ancestors as the sacred groves in India are to the priests of the Hindu and Animist religions to this day.

Merlin may have spent his time in the Forest of Caledon alone, living the life of a hermit, the defeat and carnage of Arthuret having driven him to the edge of insanity. He is sometimes portrayed as a wild man of the woods, dressed in animal skins, living off wild fruits of the forest and composing sad and prophetic poetry. In *The Apple Trees*, one

of the poems attributed to Merlin, he speaks also
of lost love:

> Sweet apple tree of lush foliage,
> I have fought beneath you to please a maiden,
> Shield on shoulder and sword on hip,
> I have slept alone in the forest of Kelyddon.
> Listen, little pig, why do you think of sleep?
> Lend your ear to the sweet song of birds.
>
> May merciless death come to me...
> Since Gwenddoleu, no prince does me honour.
> I have neither joy nor woman's company.
> At the battle of Arderyd I received a gold torque,
> And now she who is white as a swan scorns me.

Some say that towards the end of his days the
prophet, predicting his own death, sought out the
missionary St Kentigern and asked for his blessing.
In this blatant pro-Christian propaganda, Merlin –
possibly the last authentic British druid – was
converted from the ancient religion to the new.

The medieval romances, however, give us an
alternative and far more intriguing ending.
According to the legend the old wizard became
infatuated with a beautiful and fey young woman,
Nimue, who had apprenticed herself to Merlin to
learn the magic arts. Although it was only his power
she desired, she eventually gave in to his persistent
amorous advances, offering herself in exchange

for the wizard's spells, which she carefully copied
into a book as he dictated them.

The longer they travelled together the more Nimue
was repelled by this older man and when she had
extracted from him all his knowledge of wizardry,
she asked for a spell that could imprison a man
without a tower. Merlin's prophetic powers, and
what was left of his intuition, made him wary,
but she had completely beguiled him and eventually
the wizard's love for Nimue overcame his judgement
and he gave her the charm she sought.

Nimue led him to a place in the wood where the
grass grew lush and green beneath an old hawthorn
tree, and there they made love. Afterwards, Merlin
fell asleep with his head on her lap; Nimue removed
her scarf and made a ring around both the wizard
and the tree. Into this magic circle Nimue cast a
spell so powerful that even the wily wizard could
not break free from the enchantment. Thus, Merlin
became trapped forever within a hawthorn tree.

Some say that these events took place in Cadzow,
in Strathclyde; others claim it was the enchanted
Forest of Brocéliande, in Brittany. But people in
the Scottish Borders know that Merlin's hawthorn
stands near the junction of the Powsail Burn and
the River Tweed, at Drumelzier, near Broughton.
They also claim that on still nights, a person standing
in the old Drumelzier churchyard may still hear

the sound of the wizard's voice calling from within the tree.

Notes

Apples and hawthorn are undoubtedly the most common tree species to appear in Scottish traditional tales and ballads, and falling asleep beneath either was considered especially dangerous. According to the 15th century ballad, Thomas of Ercildoune fell asleep under a hawthorn known as the Eildon tree, and was taken prisoner by the Queen of Elfhame. For seven years he lived in the Otherworld before being returned to the same place. The Eildon tree is said to have lived until 1814 (showing remarkable longevity for this species), when it was blown down. At around the same time the Ercildoune estates were forfeited by the Crown, thus fulfilling one of Thomas's own prophecies: "As long as the Thorn Tree stands, Ercildoune shall keep its lands." Today a stone marks the spot on the A68.

The journey of Thomas and the Fairy Queen took a whole year and at one point they encountered an apple tree laden with fruit. Although he was hungry himself, Thomas offered the first bite of the apple to the Queen, hence passing an important test in his long initiation as a seer. When he finally left Elfhame the Queen gave him another apple and with this, the gift of prophecy for which Thomas the Rhymer is best known.

More recent authors of fairy stories have also exploited the ancient belief that the fruits of certain magical trees could confer immortality. In the Victorian romance *Lilith*, by George MacDonald (the Scots writer who is said to have influenced C.S. Lewis, Lewis Carroll and J.R.R. Tolkien), a tribe of children who never grow up survive entirely on a diet of miniature apples.

The Pursuit of Diarmuid and Grania

'An apple a day keeps the doctor away', but in the old stories, apples not only kept you healthy – they could grant immortality! In the well-known romance concerning the flight of the two young lovers Diarmuid and Grania, it was another magic tree – a rowan growing in the Wood of Dubhros – that offered the gift of eternal life. The story starts not in a wood, however, but in the banqueting hall of Fionn mac Cumhaill, the most famous warrior lord of both Scottish and Irish traditions. Fionn's noble knights and kinsmen, the Fianna, were enjoying a grand feast to celebrate the betrothal of the middle-aged Fionn to the lovely Grania, an Irish princess from Ulster, who was only half his age.

The marriage was seen by all as a good match. If Grania herself was not exactly delighted with the prospect of marrying someone old enough to be her father, she looked forward to the status gained from having such a well-loved and respected man for a husband, and so she had resigned herself to the wedding. That was until she found herself sitting opposite Diarmuid, the handsomest of all the Fianna. It was said that any woman whose eyes dwelled on Diarmuid's beautiful face would fall hopelessly in love with him. And so it was with Grania. She knew from that moment on that she could never be happy with Fionn or any other but Diarmuid.

Grania possessed a magical draught that would send any person who drank it into a deep slumber. After putting a few drops of the potion into her drinking horn, she went around the table to each person in turn, offering them a sip. Only Diarmuid was not given the sleeping draught and soon all but Grania and the object of her desire were snoring with their heads on the table.

Grania did not waste time in trying to seduce Diarmuid – she knew he would always be loyal to Fionn. Instead, she cast a spell on him that would force him to follow her wherever and howsoever she were to go. So it happened that by the time that Fionn and the Fianna awoke, Diarmuid and Grania had fled the castle to find sanctuary in the deep and lonely Wood of Dhubos.

Now, in the centre of this wood there stood a magic rowan tree that originated from a berry dropped from the hand of one belonging to the Tuatha de Danann. This huge rowan was always covered with a great many scarlet berries and eating a single fruit could confer eternal life. The Tuatha, when they realised that this rowan tree had sprung from Otherworld seed, placed it under the protection of the largest, ugliest, fiercest one-eyed giant that you would never, ever wish to meet. Needless to say nobody wanted this giant as a neighbour and the area for some distance all around the tree was a wilderness.

This was just the sort of place where the two lovers thought they would be safe from Fionn. When Diarmuid asked the one-eyed giant if he could build a hut for himself and Grania at the foot of the rowan tree, the ogre said as long as they left his precious berries alone he had no objections. So for a while Diarmuid and Grania remained safely hidden from the outside world, protected by the formidable reputation of a giant who thought nothing of having any humans who approached too close to his rowan tree for breakfast.

There they lived quite contentedly until Grania discovered she was expecting a child. Like many pregnant women she began to get terrible cravings – not for sardines, nor coal, nor baked beans, but for the fruits of the magic rowan tree. Diarmuid,

who would have gone to the ends of the earth for
Grania, tried discussing matters man to man with
the giant but when it was quite clear he was not
going to get what he wanted things turned nasty.
A bloody battle ensued and, despite the unevenness
in size, at the end of the day it was the giant who lay
bleeding to death with Diarmuid's sword through
his one eye.

Grania was delighted; now she could eat her fill of
the life-enhancing rowan berries and move from her
cramped hut into the giant's spacious tree house as
well. Thus the two young lovers settled into a life of
perfect bliss... until one day they discovered Fionn
and the whole of his mighty army camped beneath
the shade of their rowan tree. On hearing of the
demise of the giant, Fionn guessed at once that it
was his rival, Diarmuid, who had slain him and had
gone straight away to the Wood of Dhubos.

Fortunately, the tree was very large and the canopy
thick, so that Diarmuid and Grania's hiding place
was not discovered at first. From their vantage
point the lovers could see everything that was going
on below. To pass the time, Fionn had challenged
his son Ossian to a game of chess and Diarmuid,
who also happened to be a champion chess player,
watched the game with intense interest. When it
reached a critical point, when a single move could
win the game for Ossian, Diarmuid's excitement
got the better of his judgement. He dropped a single

rowan berry onto the board exactly on the square
where Ossian needed to place his chessman.
The move was made and victory gained for Ossian.
They played a second match and the same thing
happened. When Fionn lost to Ossian a third time
he was sure it must be Diarmuid's doing and he
ordered one of his men to go up into the tree to
bring the fugitive down.

Magic enters into the story again at this point.
Diarmuid was a favourite of the god Óengus
and had long enjoyed his protection. Now, in
Diarmuid's hour of need, Óengus came to his aid
again. As Fionn's man climbed the tree he was
pushed by a terrific gust of wind from its branches
and as he fell to the ground his appearance changed
to that of Diarmuid. The instant the body landed
the warriors hacked it to pieces – then watched,
horrified, as his original features returned.

Then, seeing the danger she was in, Óengus took
Grania beneath his cloak and carried her away to
safety, leaving Diarmuid alone in the tree to fend
for himself. He climbed to the topmost branches
of the rowan where he had a bird's eye view of
Fionn's army – their encampment spreading for
many leagues in every direction. To fight his way
through was clearly impossible. Diarmuid took a
deep breath and then jumped with a superhuman
leap which took him over the heads – and spears
and standards – of the Fianna, landing safely

beyond the outermost troops. It was this amazing feat that saved his life; before Fionn had realised what had happened Diarmuid had escaped into the concealment of the thick Dhubos Wood and was off to seek his beloved Grania.

Notes

Although the elopement of Diarmuid and Grania is very similar in many respects to the story of Tristan and Isolde – the reluctant bride, the seduction of the handsome but loyal kinsman, the flight to the woods, and so on – I have included both tales because of the very different roles played by the trees in each. The magic rowan tree in the Wood of Dhubos, with its fruits granting immortality, is similar to the apple trees which offer eternal youth in so many European stories (see notes under Merlin). It is perhaps worth pointing out that in the north of Britain truly wild crab apples are relatively rare whereas, by contrast, rowan is rather common.

The power of rowan against witchcraft is probably the most universal and widespread piece of tree lore in northern Europe. Certainly the people of Finland and Estonia share with people in Scotland common folk beliefs regarding rowan – hence the familiar rowan guarding the gateways of both Highland crofts and Baltic summer huts.

Bibliography

Peter Asbjørnsen (1995), *East of the Sun and West of the Moon*. Wordsworth Classics, Ware.

Alan Bruford and Donald MacDonald (1994), *Scottish Traditional Tales*. Polygon, Edinburgh.

Michael Caduto (1997), *Earth Tales*. Fulcrum, Golden, CO.

Moira Caldecott (1993), *Myths of the Sacred Tree*. Destiny Books, Rochester, VT.

Tess Darwin (1996), *The Scots Herbal*. Mercat, Edinburgh.

Robert Kirk (2006), *Secret Commonwealth of Elves, Fauns and Fairies*. New York Review of Books Classics, New York.

Cathy Low and Jackie Ross (Deeside Storytellers) (2000), *Kernunnos the Kinker*. Self-published.

Eric Maddern & Helen East (2002), *Spirit of the Forest: Tree Tales from Around the World*. Frances Lincoln, London.

Séamas Ó Catháin (1995), *The Festival of Brigit: Celtic Goddess and Holy Woman*. DBA, Dublin.

Alexander Porteous ([1928] 1996), *The Lore of the Forest*. Senate, London.

Diane Purkiss (2000), *Troublesome Things: A History of Fairies and Fairy Stories*. Allen Lane, London.

Bill Reid and Robert Bringhurst (1984), *The Raven Steals the Light*. University of Washington Press, Seattle, WA.

Stanley Robertson (1988), *Exodus to Alford*. Balnain Books, Nairn.

Francis Thompson (1978), *A Scottish Bestiary: The Lore and Literature of Scottish Beasts*. Molendinar Press, Glasgow.

Robin Williamson (1989), *The Craneskin Bag: Celtic Stories and Poems*. Canongate, Edinburgh.

Acknowledgements

Much of the research and writing for this book was done as part of a personal Millennium Award given by the Millennium Forest for Scotland in 2000. Many people were generous with their encouragement and support, especially Donald Smith, Director of the Scottish Storytelling Centre and leading light in the revival of storytelling in Scotland. Other members of the storyteller's circle have been equally forthcoming with their ideas and stories, including Linda Bandelier, Allan Davies, Helen East, John Hamilton, Donnie Henderson Shedlarz, Hugh Lupton, Barbara McDermitt, Colin Mackay, Gordon Maclellan, Claire McNicol, Eric Maddern, Daniel Morden, Senga Munro, Bob Pegg and Stanley Robertson.

I was inspired by a series of visits to northern lands that have retained their forests and their forest culture, especially Finland, Estonia, Latvia and British Columbia and I am indebted to those who tutored me on forest matters in these places, especially Argo Moor, Janis Ozolinš, Fred Puss, Hendrik Relve, Ants Viires and Nancy Turner. An essay based on my first visit to the Baltic countries was published in the Summer 2001 *Reforesting Scotland* journal.

Finally, I am very grateful to my colleagues in the RBGE and especially the publications team, Hamish Adamson, Alice Jacobs and Caroline Muir, to Eri Griffin for her superb illustrations and to the Garden's own dedicated band of storytellers, the Talking Trees.

Index of Native Trees and Other Plants